J613 Kozuszek, Jane
KOZ   Eyerly

Hygiene

DATE			
JUN 2 4 1980	SEP 2 0 1983	JUL	JUN 2 3 1998
	OCT 2 6 1983	NOV	NOV 2 7 1998
AUG 9 1980	NOV 2		
MAR 1 8 1981			FEB 1 4 2000
APR 1 4 1981	JAN 2 4 1984	FEB 5	
7/7/81	MAY 2 3	DEC 1 8	JUL 0 2 2002
JUL 2 8 1981	JUL 2 2	AUG 0 9 1994	
		JAN 2 4 1996	
OCT 2 0 1981	SEP 1	NOV 3 0 1995	
MAR 2 7 1982	FEB 6	APR 0	
OCT 2 7 1982	MAR 6	OCT 1 7 1997	
NOV 1 3 1982	MAY 9 1991	NOV 1 8	

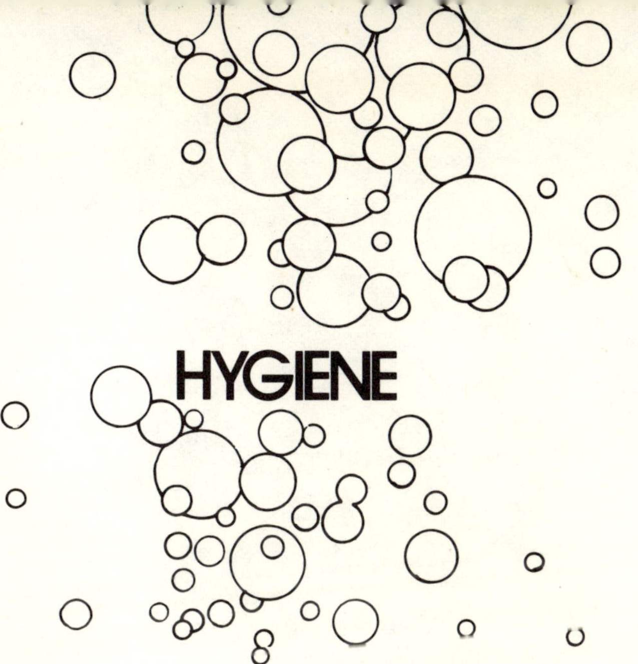

HYGIENE

BY JANE EYERLY KOZUSZEK

FRANKLIN WATTS | NEW YORK | LONDON | 1978

Cover design by Nick Krenitsky
Diagrams by Vantage Art, Inc.

Cartoon courtesy of Frank Baginski: p. 2.

Photographs courtesy of:

Center for Disease Control, Atlanta: pp. 14 (top and bottom), 34, 40 (top and bottom), 48, 55, 57, Reed and Carnrick Pharmaceutical Company: 43; Naval Dental Research Institute: p. 26 (top and bottom); New York Public Library Picture Collection: p. 21; Pfizer Inc.: p. 60.

Library of Congress Cataloging in Publication Data

Kozuszek, Jane Eyerly.
    Hygiene.

    (A First book)
    Includes index.
    SUMMARY: Presents the basic rules of good hygiene and discusses the prevention and curing of infections and illnesses.
    1. Hygiene—Juvenile literature. 2. Micro-organisms, Pathogenic—Juvenile literature. 3. Communicable diseases—Prevention—Juvenile literature. [1. Health. 2. Grooming] I. Title.
RA777.K69   613   77–16637
ISBN 0–531–01410–X

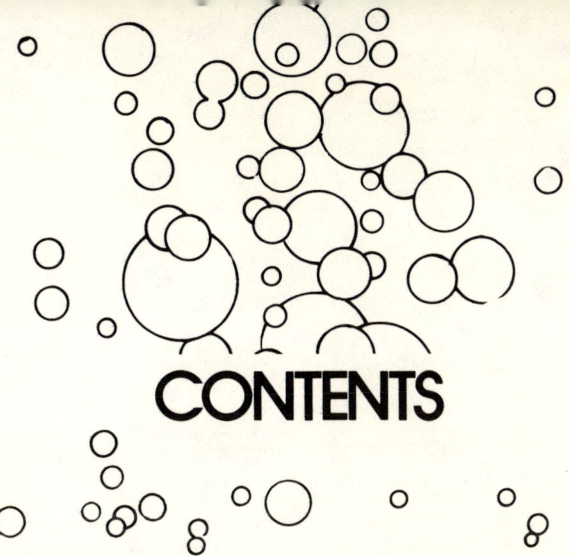

CONTENTS

The author gratefully acknowledges
the assistance of
J. Larry Harwell, M.D., pediatrician.

For assistance with "Caution in the Kitchen,"
thanks to Frank L. Bryan, Ph.D., M.P.H.,
Chief, Food-bourne Disease Training Activity,
Center for Disease Control,
U.S. Department of Health, Education, and Welfare

For assistance with "Zoo in Your Mouth,"
thanks to Patricia A. Parsons, D.D.S., M.S.,
Professor and Chairman, Department of Pedodontics,
Washington University School of Dental Medicine

WHAT'S WRONG WITH DIRT?

Soap commercials on television make dirt sound like the plague. If you buy the right product, you can wipe out that four-letter word, D-I-R-T. But is dirt always bad? The rich soil our food grows in is good. But we wash it off our hands so we don't eat chemicals or bugs. At school and play, our hands pick up other grime. When it shows, we head for the wash basin.

But even hands that don't look dirty need washing. Why? Because everything you touch—your books, your pencil, your clothes, your own skin—is covered with tiny living organisms. These organisms are so tiny, in fact, that they can be seen only through a microscope. That is why scientists call them *microorganisms*.

Among the various microorganisms is one large group called **bacteria**. Other microorganisms are **viruses** and **fungi**. Most bacteria are harmless. And some are actually helpful. They help us make bread, cheese, wine, vinegar, and some medicines, for instance. They enrich the soil, so we can grow better food. They turn animal skin to leather.

"BUT MOM, A BATH WILL DESTROY THE DELICATE ECOLOGY OF MY BODY!"

But a small number of bacteria make people sick. The word **germ** refers to any bacteria that can cause sickness, or **infection.** Some viruses and some fungi are germs too—they cause sickness.

With all these germs around us, how do we stay healthy? First, and most important, germs must get inside our bodies to do harm. If you wash your hands before eating, most of the germs will go down the drain, instead of landing on the food and going down into your stomach. When you wash a cut on your skin, you are removing germs that could get inside and breed. These are two examples of good personal **hygiene.** Hygiene is "the science of keeping healthy."

Some germs you can't control. You can't, for example, control how clean your air or water supply is. And you can't change the sanitary conditions in the dairy where your milk comes from. This area of hygiene is considered community, or public, health. It is the responsibility of government. In this book we'll be talking only about *personal* hygiene. That is, what *you* can do to stay healthy. Good hygiene can't prevent all sicknesses, of course. But it will increase your chances of staying healthy.

Aside from keeping you healthy, are there other reasons to be clean?

Body odor is not as common as television commercials would have you believe. But it can happen if you wait too long to bathe or to change your clothes. A person with body odor is usually not aware of it. People nearby are, however.

But feeling good is probably the reason most people keep clean. It feels good to clean up, especially when you are hot and sweaty. If you're tense, a warm bath is relaxing. If you're sleepy, a lukewarm shower can perk you up. And most of us feel better about ourselves when our hands, face, hair, and clothes are clean.

Following a simple hygiene program can help keep you healthier and happier. Let's take a look now at how.

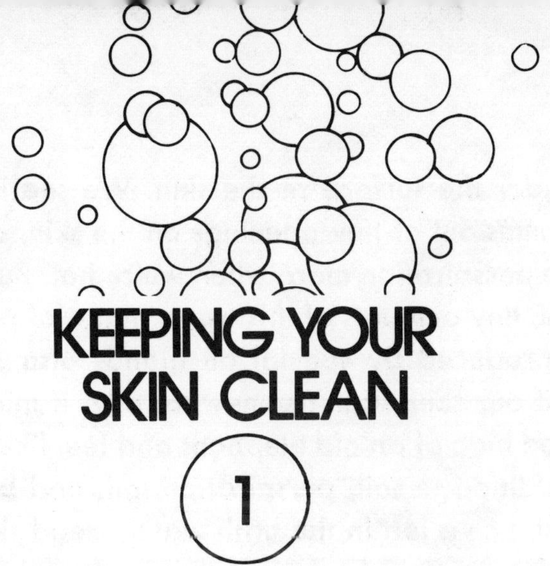

KEEPING YOUR SKIN CLEAN

Skin is an organ. In fact, it's the body's largest organ. Its main function is to protect your insides. Your body's best guard against disease germs is a healthy skin. To be healthy, skin must be kept clean. And clean skin smells good too.

WHAT YOU WASH OFF

You already know that a bath removes dirt you can see. This dirt may be soil from the playing field, pencil smudges, or remnants of food. Soap and water also remove most of the bacteria, both harmless and harmful, that live on your skin. What else comes off in the bath water? You'd be surprised!

In hot weather, or after you've been exercising, you may feel drops of water rolling down your face. When you undress at night, you may notice that your underwear and socks are slightly damp. This dampness is sweat, or **perspiration**. Perspiration is a salty waste fluid that collects in tiny glands under the surface of the skin. We see it and feel it when it comes out of tiny openings on the skin, called pores. We notice perspiration more when we're hot. But even when we're cool, tiny amounts of this waste material seep through.

Oil produced by special oil glands also seeps out of our skin. If our skin wasn't somewhat oily, it might look like the cracked hide of an old elephant and feel like sandpaper.

In addition to soil, perspiration, oil, and bacteria, one more substance is left in the bath water: dead skin cells. The skin you see on your body is dead. Underneath it are live skin cells, which grow and push the dead cells to the surface. These cells are then washed off.

A skin cell lives about twenty-eight days. Every day your body makes millions of new cells and sheds millions of dead ones. Of course you don't lose your old skin all at once, like a snake. But the skin you see today is not the skin you saw last year.

SOAP AND WATER

Soap is a combination of two main ingredients: fat and a strong alkali. The fat, also called tallow, usually comes from cows or pigs. Alkali is a salt substance obtained from the ashes of plants. When heated together, the fat reacts with the alkali. The resulting mixture is eventually hardened into various shapes.

Soap is a very effective cleaning material. When you rub your wet hands on a bar of soap, you make lather, which

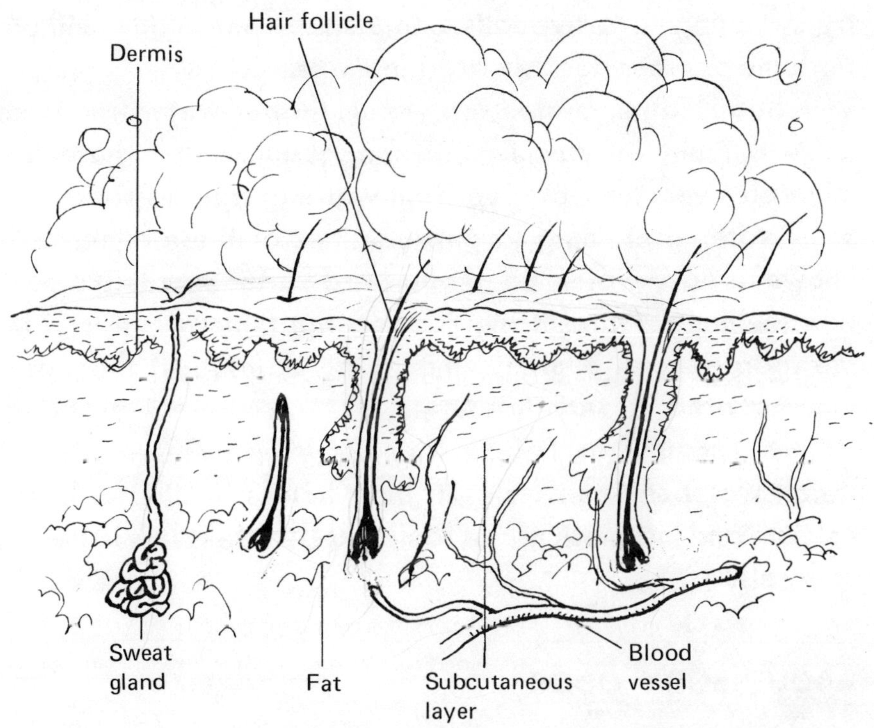

Soap and Water Bubbling Away Dirt on Skin

consists of lots of tiny bubbles. The rubbing action lifts the particles of dust, oil, sweat, dead cells, and bacteria off your skin. Then the bubbles carry them away.

All soaps sold in your local stores do a good job of getting you clean. Some brands float because they have gas or air inside them. Deodorant soaps claim to help prevent body odor. But any nondeodorant bar of soap will do the job. Sometimes perfumed soaps irritate the skin. If this happens, try switching to a hypoallergenic soap, one made without perfume or other possibly irritating ingredients.

Soaps lather best in soft water, that is, water free from large amounts of calcium and magnesium salts. These are minerals rivers may pick up from washing against rocks and soil. Water containing large quantities of these minerals is known as hard water. Soap and hard water may leave your skin feeling dry and itchy. Further, the minerals react with the soap to form a grimy ring in the bathtub. If the water in your area is very hard, the water company probably softens it somewhat. People who like even softer water can install water-softener tanks in their homes. In the tank, the calcium and magnesium are replaced by other, less irritating minerals.

ABOUT BODY ODOR

Perspiration is usually blamed for body odor. However, the odor actually comes from the combination of perspiration, oil, bacteria, dead skin cells, and dirt. The longer this mixture remains on your body, the more noticeable the odor gets. In hot weather, especially, it doesn't take too long for your skin, and you, to smell bad.

Body odor can come from any part of the body. However, certain parts are more likely to smell than other parts. Your feet always perspire a lot because they are enclosed in shoes. Thus, feet and socks quickly get a distinctive odor. This odor can be removed only by soap and water. Since it is not exposed to much air, the area between your legs where your reproductive organs are located, called the genital area, is another place likely to acquire an odor. Daily washing plus wearing clean underwear and socks will keep these parts of you smelling good.

Many garments worn today are of man-made fibers such as polyester or nylon. These fibers are tightly woven. They don't let the perspiration evaporate as easily as cotton fibers do. The resulting odor can be unpleasant. Avoid it by changing your slacks, shirts, tops, and dresses every day or two.

Underarm Body Odor

One kind of odor gets a lot of publicity—underarm odor. The underarm areas have regular sweat glands, like the rest of your skin. They also have a special type of gland that is triggered by emotional excitement instead of heat or exercise. When perspiration from this area mixes with skin bacteria, it produces a distinctive smell, different from regular sweat.

In young children, the special sweat glands have not yet begun to operate. Girls will first notice the distinctive underarm odor around the time of their first menstrual period (see pp. 17–18). Boys will notice the odor at varying ages, depending upon their individual sexual development. Sometimes a daily bath and change of clothes will prevent noticeable odor. If not, you can try a deodorant or an antiperspirant.

Antiperspirants reduce the flow of sweat. They also contain ingredients that stop bacteria from growing. Deodorants don't stop the sweat, but they do cut down on the number of odor-producing bacteria. Both products can cause skin irritation, which can lead to infection. Sometimes the basic ingredients are to blame. Other times the irritation comes from the perfume, or, in an aerosol product, from the propellant. Some doctors find that antiperspirants, especially the extra-dry types, cause more skin problems than do deodorants, which are milder.

Both products come in a confusing number of forms: cream, stick, roll-on, aerosol, and non-aerosol spray. Whichever kind you select, remember to use it *after*, not *instead of*, soap and water.

IN THE TUB OR SHOWER

Some people enjoy soaking in a warm bath. Others prefer the sharp sting of a shower. Whichever you like, be sure to soap your body well. Pay special attention to the feet, genital area, and around the ears. A washcloth is useful because the rubbing action helps loosen dead skin cells.

Bubble bath is fun to use, but many doctors believe it can be harmful. A detergent, similar to the kind used to wash clothes, is responsible for the bubbles. The harsh chemicals in bubble baths have been blamed for several types of skin irritation. Also, the detergent can irritate a girl's vaginal opening or get inside her bladder and actually burn it. Bath oil does not usually irritate, but may clog the pores. Instead, try using an after-bath lotion, especially on the elbows, knees, and feet, to give your skin a silky smooth feeling.

HOW OFTEN TO BATHE?

This depends on the weather and on how active you are. In hot, humid weather, you perspire more. You also perspire a great deal if you take part in sports, summer or winter. In these situations, daily bathing is a good idea.

In winter, bathing for nonathletes every day is not really necessary and, in fact, may make your skin too dry. The warm, dry air from indoor heating dries out skin, and too much soap and water may make it feel uncomfortable. Bathing every other day or even less often may be enough. However, you should wash your face, hands, and genital area daily.

DRY UP

After soaping and rinsing carefully, rub your body dry with a clean towel. Fresh oil will flow from the oil glands to keep your skin soft. Proper drying helps prevent some skin infections discussed later.

After you bathe or shower, hang up your washcloth and towel to dry. If they lie in a heap for hours, they will stay damp and eventually begin to smell. The odor comes from **mildew** being formed on the moist fabric. Mildew is produced by a fungus. Sometimes you can see mildew in the form of dark spots. Keeping your towel and your washcloth dry between washings will stop the growth of any fungi.

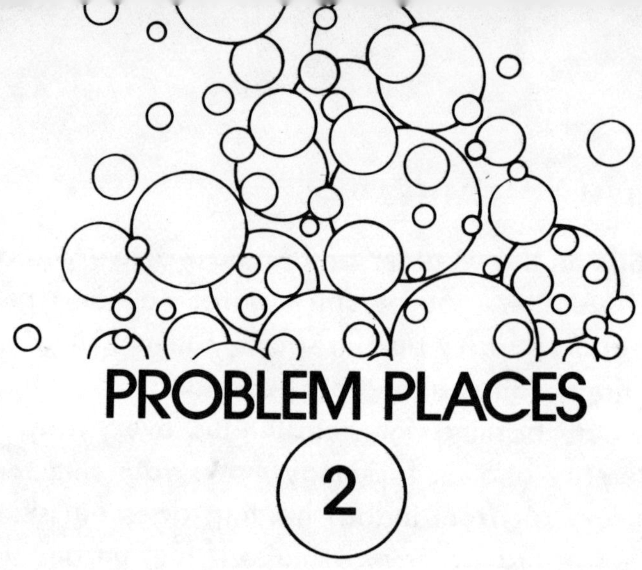

PROBLEM PLACES

2

Infection occurs when harmful microorganisms invade your body. Certain places on your body are more likely to develop infections than other places. But you can avoid most or even all if you pay special attention to these trouble spots.

HAND TO MOUTH

Of all parts of your body, your hands need the most frequent washing. Think of all the things your hands touch each day—the toilet, your shoes, your jacket, the bus seat, the school door handle, books, pencils, your desk. And did the same hands, which picked up all those bacteria and perhaps other tiny organisms, then rub your eyes or pick your nose or grab a sandwich?

Since hands come into contact with so many microorganisms, we call them the "carriers of infection." If you have certain germs on your hands when you eat, the germs may go onto the food and then into your stomach, possibly causing stomachache, vomiting, or diarrhea. Rubbing your eyes with bacteria-covered fingers may infect the delicate inner lining of the eyelid. This contagious infection is called **conjunctivitis,** or pinkeye. It usually can be prevented by frequent hand washing and by keeping your hands away from your eyes.

If no soap is around, wash anyway. Many germs can be removed by rubbing your hands together under running water and then against a clean towel. Most of the germs (although not all the dirt) will go down the drain.

When should hands be washed? Important times are: before you prepare food or eat it; after you use the toilet; before you go to bed; and any other time they look dirty. Washing after using the toilet is especially important. Even a healthy person's bowel movements have germs. A sick person's may carry many more. A healthy person's urine should be free of germs. But bacteria can flourish in drops of urine that remain on your body or on a toilet seat. This makes it doubly important to wash after using a school or other public toilet that many people use.

Fingernails need special attention. Nasty bacteria known as **staphylococci** (staph, for short) can hide under fingernails and infect a pimple or mosquito bite you've scratched. Fingernails should be kept fairly short. They're stronger and easier to keep clean. Cut nails with special small scissors and file them with a nail file or emery board. Using a fingernail brush to clean under them is a good idea.

When you dry your hands, push back the cuticle (the

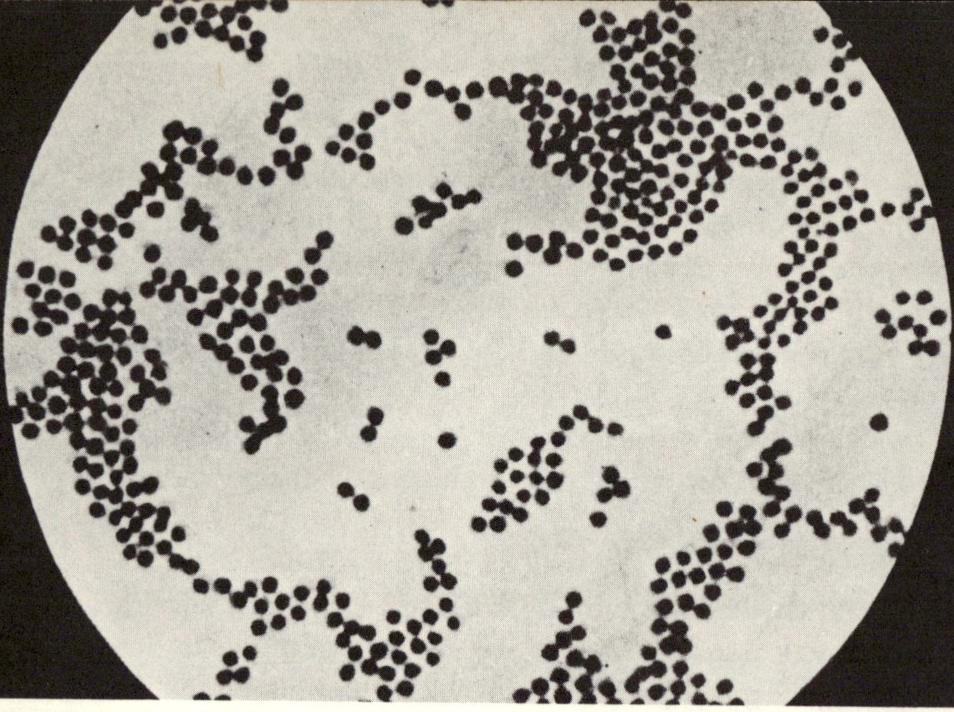

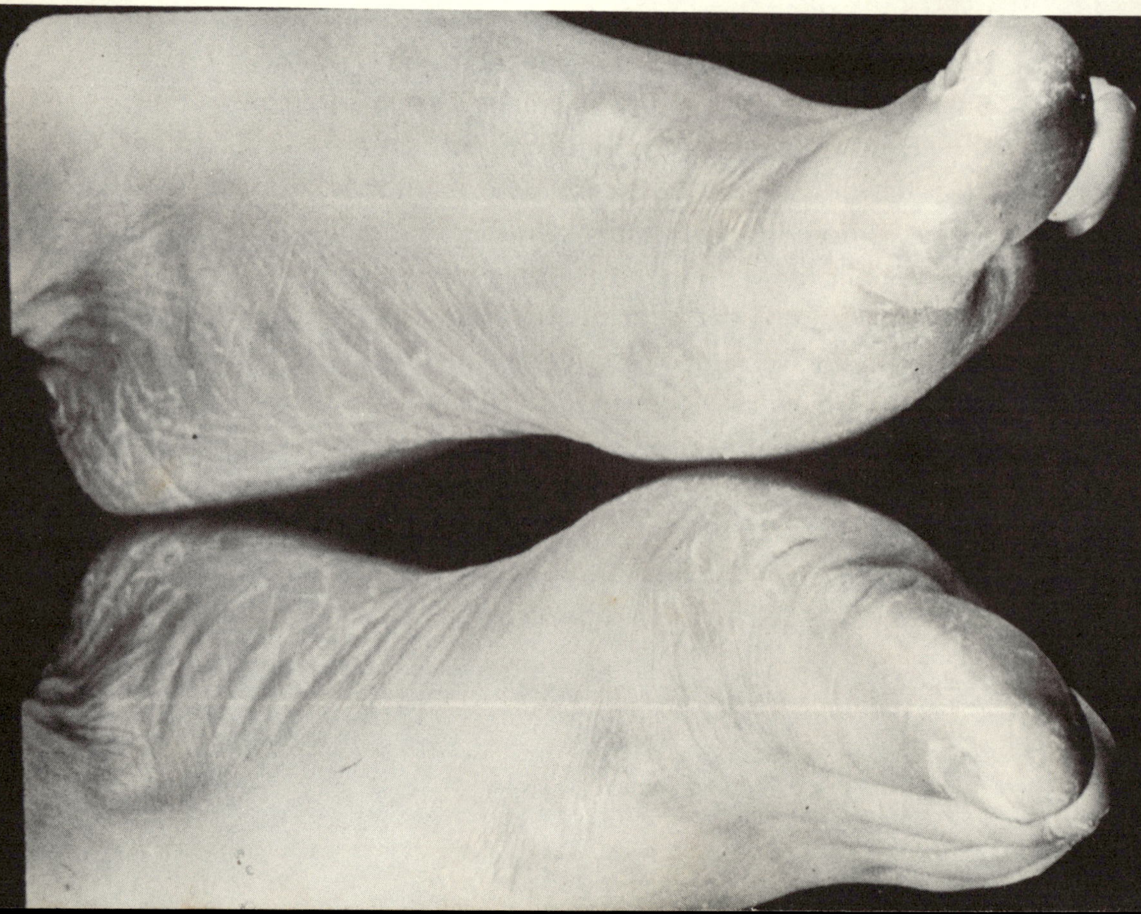

hardened skin around the base of the fingernail) with a towel. This helps prevent hangnails, which are torn bits of cuticle. Hangnails that are picked until they bleed may become infected, especially if your hands are dirty most of the time.

BEST FOOT FORWARD

Germs need warmth and moisture to grow. Since feet perspire more than some other body parts, remember to keep them clean and dry. Damp feet can develop a skin infection called **athlete's foot**, caused by **ringworm** fungi growing between the toes. Signs of athlete's foot are redness, dampness, and pain between the toes.

To avoid athlete's foot, always wear socks, even with gym shoes. Socks absorb foot moisture and so the foot stays drier. Change socks daily or more often if they get damp. Never wear other people's shoes or socks. When you bathe or swim, dry your feet carefully, including the spaces between the toes. And always wear rubber thongs, or clogs, in public showers and locker rooms, where the fungus can easily be picked up from the floor.

If you get athlete's foot, try to keep your feet dry by following the rules just mentioned. Ask your druggist to sug-

Above: staphylococcus bacteria, greatly enlarged.
Below: ringworm on the feet, or athlete's feet.

gest a cream or powder. If these do not clear up the infection, your doctor can give you a prescription for an ointment or foot powder.

Another type of foot infection is caused by **yeasts.** Yeasts are also members of the fungus family. Yeast infections can start if the feet become irritated by chemicals or glues used in some shoes. With a yeast infection, the tops and tips of the toes get red and very itchy. Wearing clean socks makes yeast infections less likely. Socks also help you avoid foot blisters, which can get infected easily.

Sometimes infections start from ingrown toenails. Cutting the nails straight across will usually prevent them from growing down into the skin.

BOTTOMS UP

If you feel sore around the anus (the opening for bowel movements), it could be a sign that you need to bathe more often. Or perhaps you're not rinsing or drying yourself well. It's also possible you are not doing a good job of wiping after a bowel movement. Some doctors recommend a pre-moistened tissue sold for this purpose. Girls should always wipe in one direction, toward their back. This keeps the bowel movement out of the vaginal opening.

It's just about impossible to wipe away every trace of waste matter. Frequent baths or showers are the best way to keep clean. Changing underwear daily is also important.

Boys especially need to carefully wash and dry the

genital area. Otherwise they can get a fungus infection called **jock itch** (also sometimes called Dhobi itch). The infection gets its name from the jockstrap, an elasticized supporter that men sometimes wear to protect themselves. A dirty, damp jockstrap also can chafe and irritate the genital area.

Bathing daily is also important when a girl begins to menstruate. **Menstruation** can begin anytime between the ages of nine and sixteen, but usually starts between eleven and fourteen. Each month, a tiny egg cell is released from one of the girl's two ovaries. Ovaries are almond-sized glands in the abdomen. At about the same time the egg is released, the lining of a girl's uterus grows extra cells. If the egg is fertilized (united with a male sperm), it will tuck itself into the thickened lining of the uterus and begin to grow. The girl will be pregnant. The extra cells provide nourishment in the early stages of the unborn baby's development.

If the egg is not fertilized, the uterus casts off the extra cells and extra blood in a fluid called the menstrual flow. This fluid passes from the uterus out of the vaginal opening. Though the flow can last from three to seven days, it actually amounts to only a few ounces worth. Once menstruation becomes regular, it usually takes place about once a month.

To absorb the menstrual flow, girls wear disposable pads called sanitary napkins, or they wear tampons. Some napkins are held in place against the body by sticky tape that presses against regular underpants. Others require special panties or belts. Most sanitary napkins stop up plumb-

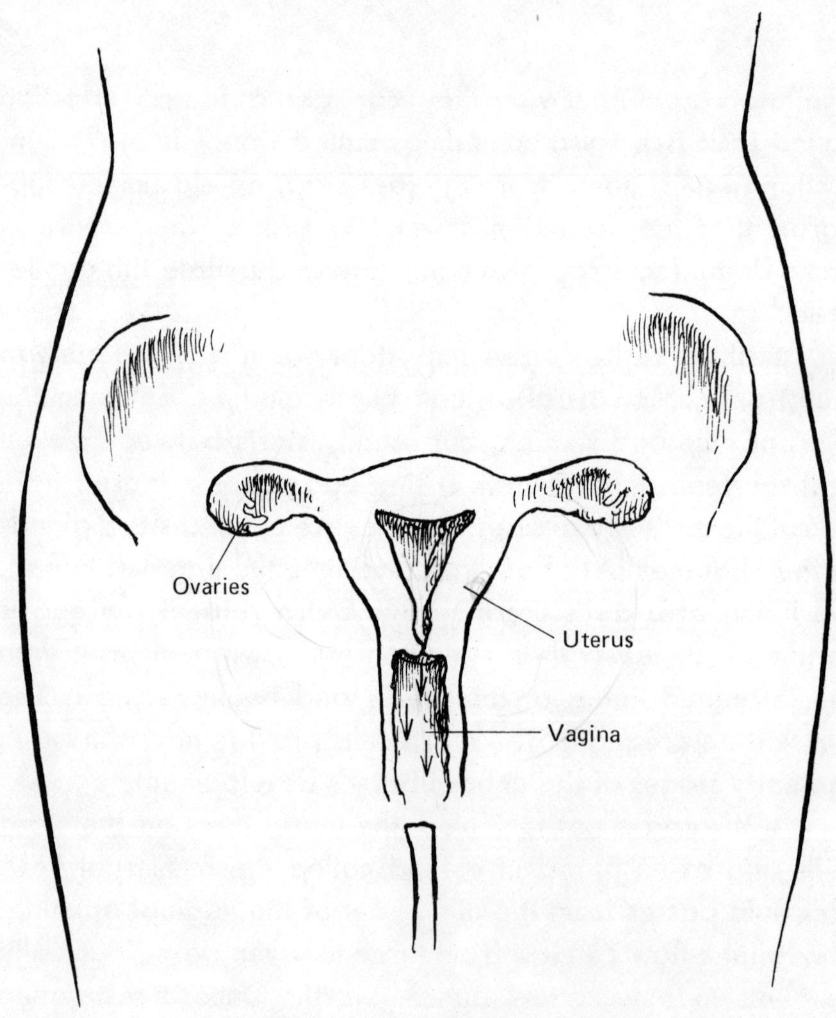

ing if they are flushed down the toilet. Check the package to see. They should be wrapped in several layers of toilet tissue and placed in a wastebasket. Public toilets have metal containers with lids for this purpose.

Tampons are slim rolls of cotton that are inserted into the vagina and worn internally. They are easy to dispose of since they can be safely flushed down the toilet. However, some doctors and parents do not believe young girls should use tampons.

The menstrual fluid gets a disagreeable odor after it is exposed to bacteria in the air. For this reason, it's important to bathe daily and change the sanitary pad often. Once a girl has begun having menstrual periods (or perhaps a few months earlier), she will notice that her underarm area perspires more. The perspiration itself will have a definite odor. If daily use of soap and water does not stop noticeable odor, a deodorant product may also be used.

HAIR CARE

Hair collects dirt quickly. Brushing it ten or twelve strokes a day will remove some surface dirt. A weekly washing is usually necessary to keep it looking and smelling good. Regular soap can leave a soapy film on your hair. Shampoo products work the best. They usually consist of a detergent wetting agent, a water softener, and perhaps a perfume.

Before you wet your hair, brush it well to remove loose dirt, dead cells, and tangles. Then let your brush and comb soak in soapy water for a few minutes. Wet your hair and work in a small amount of shampoo. Rub your scalp briskly with your fingertips and then rinse with plenty of warm water. A second application of shampoo produces more lather because there is less oil and dirt in the hair. But a single application is usually enough.

Some shampoos have ingredients that are supposed to improve the look and feel of your hair. Protein shampoos (made from the cartilage and joints of cows or pigs) can make thin hair look thicker, but the same product weighs down oily hair. Egg shampoos have no special value. Eggs have protein, but not the kind that helps hair. Some herbal shampoos may irritate the scalp or cause allergic reactions. A shampoo with lemon juice is good for oily hair, but lemon *juice* has to be in it, not just a lemon smell.

Hair conditioners also come in a variety of types. They are applied after shampooing and then rinsed out. Most people don't find them helpful, but some do. Cream rinses contain chemicals that can soften dry or bushy hair, making it easier to comb and keep in place. But the same rinse can make other types of hair go limp. Protein conditioners work like protein shampoos, coating thin hair to make it appear thicker. If you have oily hair, you can make your own rinse from one lemon and a cup of warm water. Squeeze the lemon halves, strain, mix with the water, and work into the hair. Then rinse out.

Sometimes hair needs more than a weekly washing. This is true if your skin is extra oily, or if you notice white flakes in your hair or on your shoulders. These flakes are

An advertisement for shampoo
in the early 1900s.

Systematic Shampooing

"Young Americans who do not wish to lose their hair before they are forty, must begin to look after their scalps before they are twenty."

New York Medical Record.

With Packer's Tar Soap means healthy hair and scalp—and you cannot begin too early. To get the best results, specify

PACKER'S

Our Leaflet:—"The Value of Systematic Shampooing," sent free. Address
THE PACKER MANUFACTURING CO. (Suite 878X), 81 Fulton Street, New York.

dead skin cells from your scalp. Everyone has them, but when they are large and easy to see the condition is called **dandruff**. Although dandruff is embarrassing and annoying, it is not a sickness. It can't be "caught" from another person. If you have it, it probably won't go away. But it can be helped. Several good nonprescription dandruff shampoos are available. If necessary, ask your doctor for a suggestion. Sometimes dandruff isn't caused by a scalp condition. The flakes could be the result of lack of brushing, poor shampooing, or not enough rinsing. In these cases, proper hair care should solve the problem.

ABOUT FACE

Your face and neck should be washed every morning and night. Your neck probably needs soap. Until your teen years, however, your face may not need soap every day unless there is dirt or grease on it that water alone won't remove.

When you wash your face, wipe out the inside of your ears with a finger wrapped in a warm wet washcloth. Don't worry about dirt or ear wax you can't reach with your finger. Cotton-tipped toothpicks can be dangerous. They pack the wax into the ear and can even poke a hole in your eardrum. No object smaller than a finger should ever go into your ear.

You may notice some blemishes on your face. These are a result of extra oil your body is producing. Blackheads and whiteheads are plugs of dried oil. Picking either one can cause infection and produce a larger and more painful

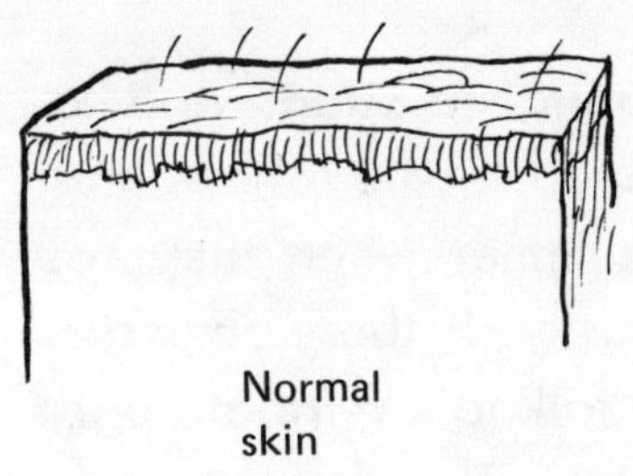

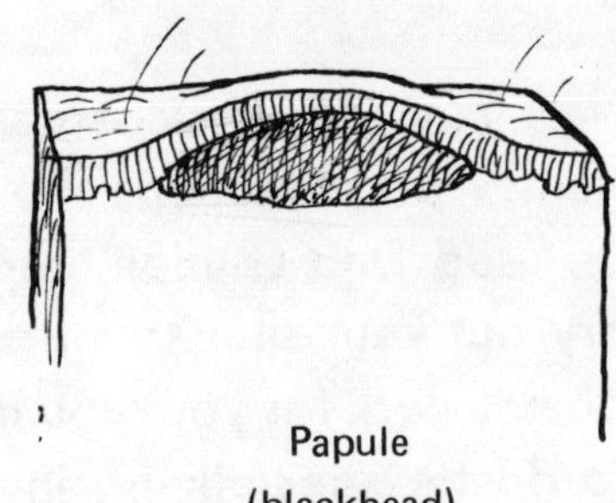

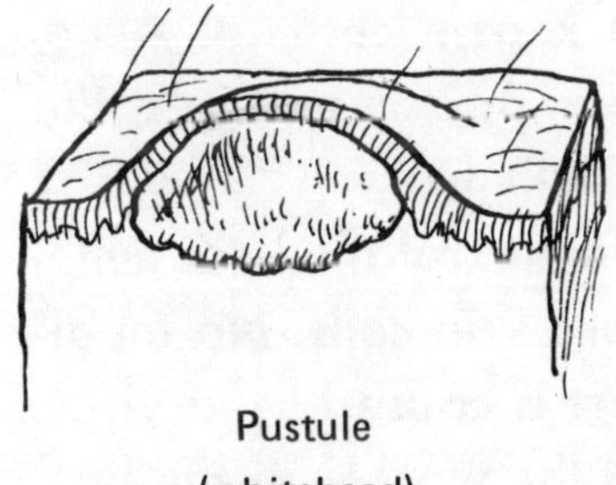

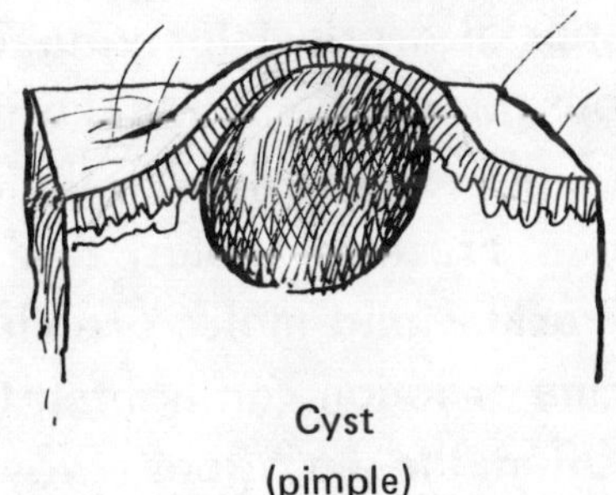

blemish called a pimple. Whiteheads sometimes get infected and turn into pimples even without picking.

A person with these skin disorders has what is called acne. Certain foods were once believed to cause it. Anxiety, lack of cleanliness, and constipation have also been blamed. Now doctors believe that oily skin is the principal cause.

If you have acne, you should keep your face and hands as clean as you can. Your goal is to get rid of as much extra oil as possible. Washing your hands is important too, since they touch your face often and even clean fingers carry some oil. Also, staph bacteria from your fingers may infect blackheads and whiteheads.

Your pharmacist can suggest antiacne soaps and lotions. Abrasive soaps should not be used. Some lotions must be used with caution, especially in summer when they can dry out your skin so much it burns easily. If these remedies do not work for you, you may want to talk to a dermatologist (a doctor specializing in skin problems). The dermatologist can analyze your skin and have the pharmacist make up a special product for you. There is no known cure for acne, but good care can make it milder. As a person matures, the oil glands usually stop their excessive activity.

Freckles, moles, and warts have no relation to acne. Freckles and moles are clusters of dark skin cells. No medicine or lotion can lighten them. A wart is caused by a virus. Often, the wart goes away by itself. If the wart is on the bottom of your foot (called a plantar wart) or if it bothers you, see a doctor. Picking at moles or warts can infect them.

ZOO IN YOUR MOUTH

Probably the first person to see bacteria was a Dutchman named Anton van Leeuwenhoek. More than three hundred years ago, soon after the microscope was invented, he scraped a tiny bit of matter from one of his teeth and looked at it under the microscope. To his surprise, he saw tiny moving creatures that he called "animalcules."

These animalcules were some of the thousands of bacteria that always live in our mouth. Some are harmless. Others cause **cavities**, also called tooth decay. Large groups of the harmful bacteria live together on the thin, sticky layer covering your teeth called plaque. The bacteria eat bits of food left on the teeth and produce an acid. The result is a cavity, or hole. To repair a cavity, the dentist first removes decayed parts of the tooth and then puts in a metal or plastic filling.

A clean tooth will not decay. As long as any food bits remain on your teeth, the bacteria can produce damaging acid. Foods such as cakes, biscuits, cookies, ice cream, caramel popcorn, and chewing gum encourage the flow of acid more than other foods do. As you chew, the sugar and flour from these foods form a sticky paste that clings to your teeth. Soda pop is bad too, but it doesn't linger on the teeth for as long a time as other sweets.

Try to limit sweets to mealtime. Then brush. Between meals, eat snacks that don't start the acid flowing. Fruit causes less acid production than sweets. But best of all for teeth are nuts, popcorn, cheese, and any raw vegetable. These foods cause the smallest amount of acid production.

When to Brush
"Brush after every meal" is a rule that is often broken. But it is still the best way to have a clean mouth. Brushing after breakfast has two advantages: it removes food from the teeth, and it removes those little fur coats you may feel on your teeth when you wake up. Before going to bed, however, is the *most* important time to brush. When you sleep, your saliva production goes down. This means that any food on

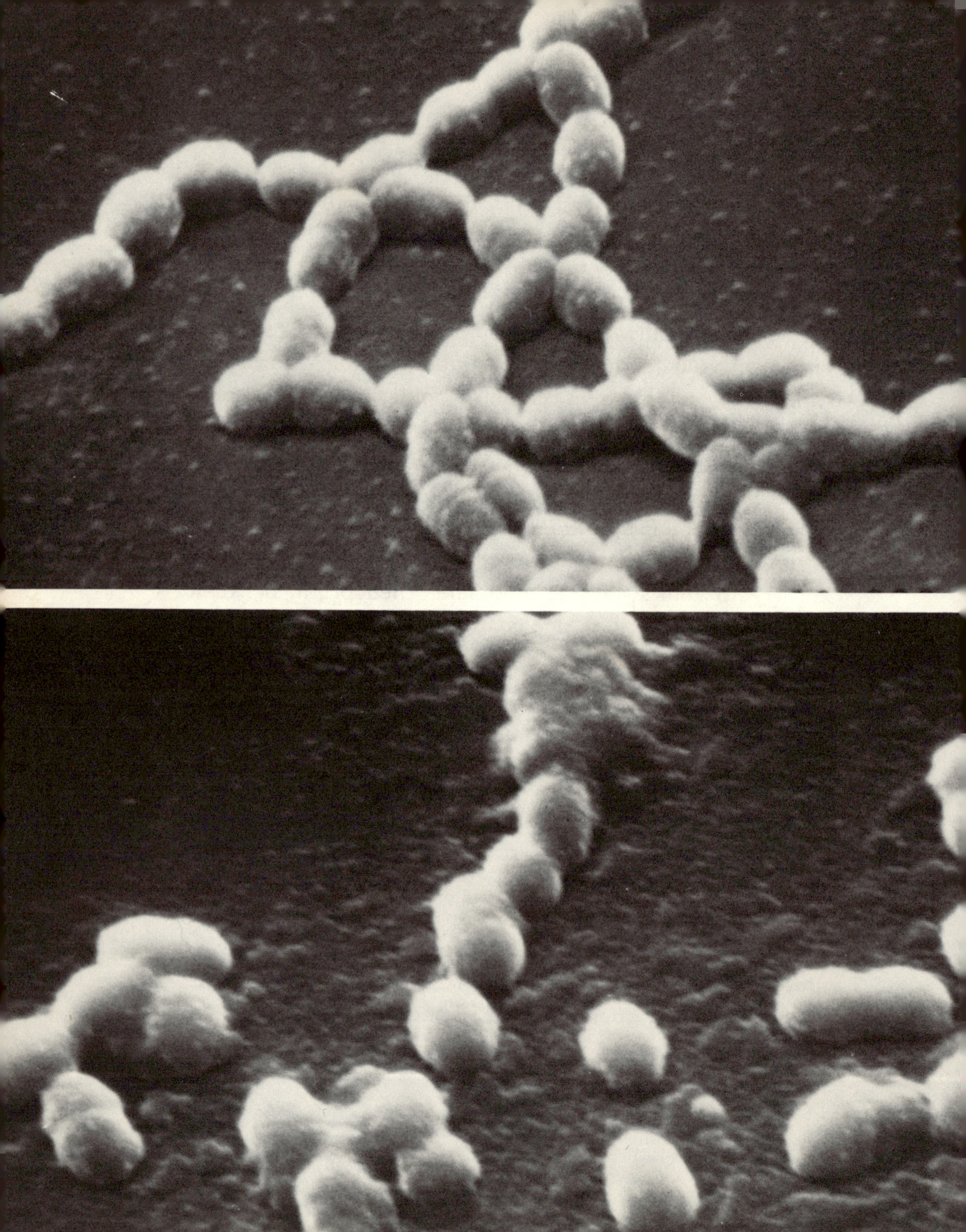

your teeth when you fall asleep will not be washed away, and will stay there until morning.

Tools for Brushing

An ordinary toothbrush, *properly used,* does at least as good a job as an electric one. Since soft bristles wear out quickly, replace your brush every two months. Many dentists like a multi-tufted soft nylon brush. Flat bristles (not angled or curved) are usually recommended. Water jet devices should not be used without a dentist's recommendation. They are rarely necessary. And high water pressure can even damage the gum tissue.

Your toothbrush can't clean the spaces between your teeth. For this job you need dental floss, a special thread sold in pharmacies. Unless told otherwise by your dentist, choose the unwaxed kind. Your dentist should show you how to guide the floss gently between the teeth. Move to a clean place on the floss each time you move to a different tooth. You'll be surprised to see how many tiny bits of food the floss removes. Flossing does two other jobs: it cleans below the gum line between the teeth, and it removes plaque from the sides of teeth. Flossing can be done either before or after brushing.

Above: bacteria on healthy teeth.
Below: bacteria damage
on teeth coated with sugar.

Toothpastes are alike in many ways, but some contain a very important ingredient that helps prevent tooth decay— fluoride. Fluoride is a chemical found in rocks, earth, some water, and in bones and teeth. A toothpaste with fluoride is the best choice.

Other ingredients in toothpastes are an abrasive (polishing agent) to clean the enamel, a synthetic detergent (foaming agent) to loosen and help remove surface stains, and other substances that give body to the toothpaste and prevent it from drying out. Finally, a special flavoring is added so you'll enjoy using the product.

Commercial toothpaste (or powder) makes brushing pleasant and leaves the mouth with a fresh taste. But it's the brushing, not the toothpaste, that does the real cleaning.

How to Brush

Brushing your teeth removes food and some of the bacteria. It also massages and stimulates the gums. This makes them healthier and more resistant to gum disease. It takes about three minutes to brush the teeth and gums well. Here's how to do it:

1. *Outside surfaces.* Bite the front teeth together. Then scrub the exposed top and bottom front teeth back and forth, up and down, many times. Brush the gums too. Moving your brush back on one side, scrub the outsides of those teeth, top and bottom. Then repeat on the other side.
2. *Inside surfaces.* Open your mouth and scrub the inside surfaces of the top teeth and then the bottom teeth. It takes

longer to do a good job inside, since it's hard to get to all the corners.

3.   *Finish* by brushing the chewing surfaces of the top and bottom teeth.

A "disclosing tablet" (from your dentist or druggist) can tell you how effective your brushing and flossing is. To disclose means to expose to view. After you think your teeth are clean, chew the tablet. You probably will find parts of your teeth are stained red. This dye shows up only where plaque remains. To remove the stain, brush and floss again. By checking yourself, you learn what areas you are neglecting.

Bad Breath

Another word for bad breath is halitosis. Halitosis can make a person lose friends. One cause is a mouth that needs brushing and flossing. Sometimes food will collect in the many grooves on the back of the tongue and cause the breath to smell bad. Daily brushing stops this kind of bad breath.

Sometimes sickness causes bad breath. If you have a bad head cold or sinus trouble (sinuses are the cavities in the skull above the eyes), the mucus dripping down the throat, called postnasal drip, can smell bad. This kind of bad breath can be masked but not eliminated by breath deodorizers from a drugstore.

Still another cause of bad breath is decaying teeth and unhealthy gums. If you are taking care of your teeth and see a dentist at least once a year, you probably won't have bad breath from this cause.

PREVENTING INFECTION FROM SKIN BREAKS

3

Your skin is your body's best protection against unfriendly germs. What happens when this natural barrier is broken by a cut, scratch, or burn? The moment your skin is broken, millions of bacteria that live on your skin have a chance to get inside.

KEEP OUT GERMS

Any skin break should be washed immediately with plain soap and water. Washing gets rid of germs before they can enter, breed, and cause an infection. Soap and water work far better than antiseptics sold to kill germs. The chemicals in antiseptics can sometimes even damage your skin cells.

Exposure to air will help a wound heal faster. Germs grow best in moist, warm places. A bandage does more harm than good if it's keeping your cut moist. Use one if it's really necessary, but be sure to take it off at night and let the area dry out. Although constant exposure to moisture is bad, a wound should be washed several times a day with soap and water and then carefully patted dry.

FIRST AID TIPS

•   *If your skin is scratched or cut,* wash your injury (even if it's tiny) with soap and water. If you have no soap, use plenty of water. Then pat the area with a clean towel or dry it in the air. Air is cleaner than a used towel! If your cut is bleeding heavily, get help. If the cut is bleeding only slightly or not at all, press gently around the edges (with clean fingers) to encourage a little bleeding. This will help remove bits of dirt or glass that may have gotten inside.

•   *If you get a puncture wound,* be on the alert. Puncture wounds caused by sharp objects such as nails may not bleed, but can be very serious. The sharp object may carry the very dangerous bacteria that cause the disease **tetanus** (also called lockjaw). Tetanus can be fatal! If you get a puncture wound, see a doctor. You may need a tetanus booster shot to prevent your getting this dread disease.

•   *If you get a splinter,* try to remove it with tweezers or ask the school nurse or someone else to help you. Wash your hands well first. If you are using a needle to dig out a splinter, hold the needle in a match flame for a second or two. This will kill most of the germs. After the splinter is removed, wash the area with soap and water. A tetanus booster shot may also be recommended here.

• *If you have a mild burn,* soak the burned area in cold water immediately, for about ten minutes. Add ice cubes to keep it cold. If your burn forms a blister or hurts a great deal, cover it lightly with a sterile bandage or clean handkerchief. Then get help from a professional medical person.

• *If you get a blister,* wash the blister but don't pop it. A blister on your foot may come from wearing shoes without socks or shoes that are too small. Try to break in new shoes by wearing them for an hour at a time, until they stretch a little.

• *If you get a sunburn.* Too much sun is not good for your skin. It can even lead to skin cancer later on. Excessive sun and sunlamps also make the skin look old before it should. Use a sun screening lotion before you swim, play tennis, or work in the sun. If you get a bad burn, see your doctor. Serious sunburns can cause infection.

INFECTED WOUNDS

Sometimes, in spite of your best efforts, your skin will get infected. Skin infections do not always begin with an injury. They can also occur if you don't bathe enough.

How can you tell if your wound is infected? One warning sign is a blister filled with a yellowish liquid called **pus.** When enemy bacteria enter your wound, your body's own defense system springs into action. The white blood cells always present in your blood rush to the scene. Their purpose is to stop the invading bacteria from multiplying. Pus contains dead bacteria and white blood cells.

Sometimes white blood cells can't control the invading germs. When this happens, the infection gets worse. Some warning signs of a *serious* infection are redness, red streaks, swelling, tenderness, and heat. If any of these signs is present or if the wound is draining a cloudy fluid, see a nurse or doctor.

COMMON SKIN INFECTIONS

One common skin infection is **impetigo.** Impetigo can start when dirty hands scratch a mosquito bite or a cut. Then certain kinds of bacteria can get into your body and multiply. First, the skin forms small, itchy blisters. Then scabs appear. If you scratch the impetigo, the infection can spread to other parts of your body or to other people.

Sometimes the impetigo will go away if you wash often with soap and water. Washing softens the scabs, which can then be peeled off. (This is one scab that it's all right to pick!) Impetigo itself is not serious. However, it can lead to serious kidney problems if the infection gets into the bloodstream. For this reason, get medical advice if it doesn't clear up in a few days.

A **boil** is a serious and painful skin infection. A boil starts when staph bacteria begin to grow on the skin in an opening where the hair comes out. The area becomes puffy

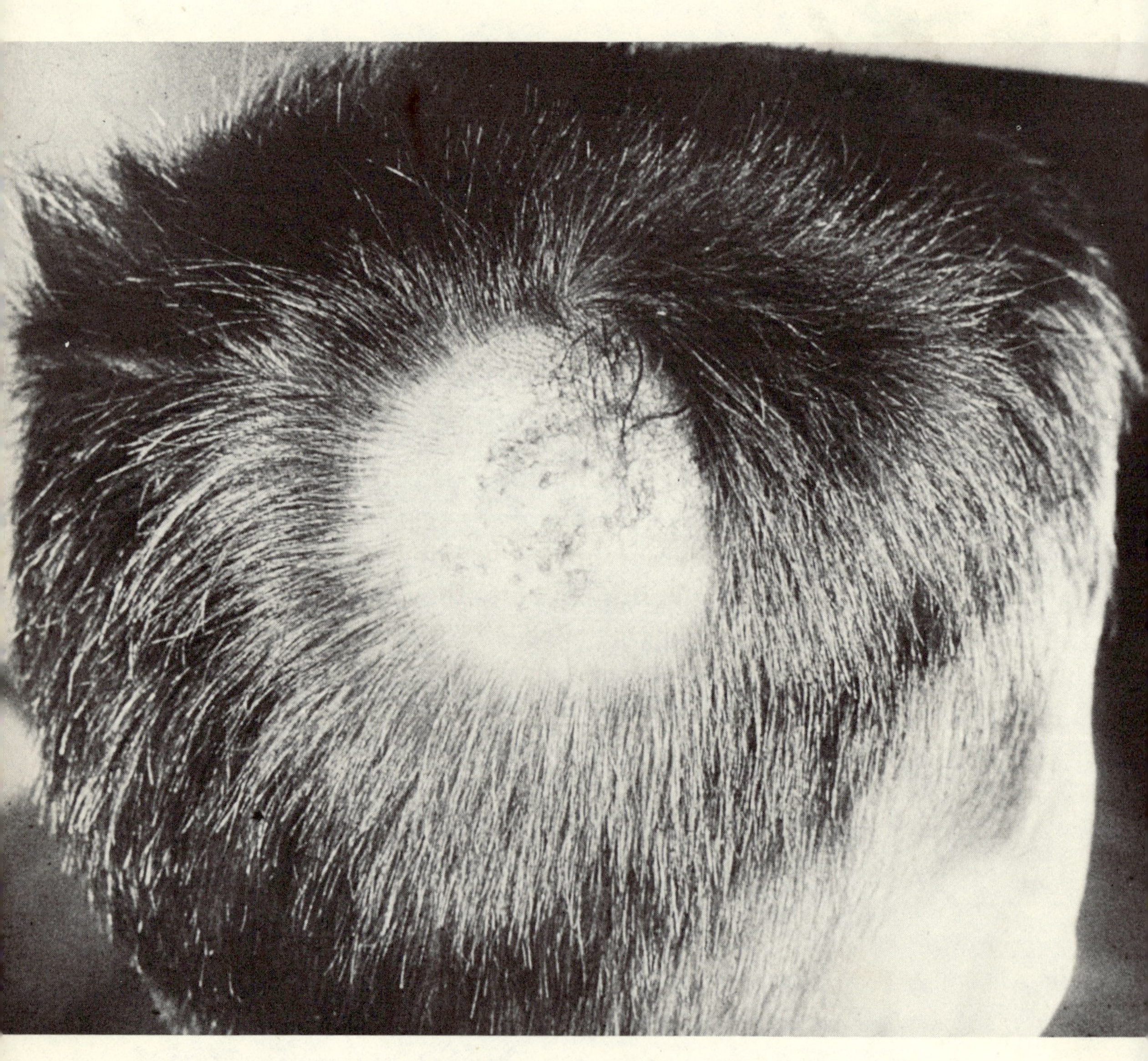

Ringworm on the scalp

with pus. A **sty** is similar, but it is located on the eyelid. It can start when you rub your dirty fingers in your eye. Boils and sties need professional medical attention.

All skin infections do not start with bacteria. Another microorganism, fungus, is responsible for ringworm. With ringworm, the middle of your sore heals first, producing a ringlike appearance. Ringworm on the scalp or skin needs a doctor's attention. Ringworm on the feet is athlete's foot. When the ringworm fungus grows on a boy's genital area, it is called jock itch, referred to earlier.

ASK AN EXPERT

Whenever you have an injury or a skin condition that does not seem to heal, see a doctor or nurse. Many infections can be healed only with medicine prescribed by a doctor. And a small infection left to itself can get worse and make your whole body sick.

PROTECTING YOURSELF FROM OTHER INFECTIONS

4

Soap and water are your basic weapons against skin infections. But other diseases can be prevented in other ways. Sometimes you can avoid a serious disease by following a few simple hygiene rules. For instance, do you know why you shouldn't drink water from a stream when you are camping?

BEWARE OF THE WATER

Perhaps you are camping or hiking and you run low on water. You see clean-looking water in a lake, river, or stream. But beware: the water may be unsafe. You should boil it for twenty minutes to kill any germs present. Various disease germs may have spread to the water from nearby sewers. If you drink unclean water or swim in it, you may get sick.

Pouring sewage into the river (or even into the gutter) used to be common. People had no idea that body waste products could contain germs that spread disease. Today, sewage is not allowed to reenter the water supply without being filtered and partly cleaned. The drinking water from your tap has undergone a complex process of purification to remove all these disease germs. Lake and river water has not.

DIRTY NEEDLES

A kind of hepatitis (a liver-damaging disease), called **serum hepatitis**, is carried on dirty hypodermic needles. The disease gets its name because the germ is carried through the body in the part of blood known as the serum. If a girl with serum hepatitis gets her ears pierced and the same needle is then used on your ears, you probably will get the disease. Ears should be pierced only by professional medical personnel. Serum hepatitis is quite common among users of illegal drugs. The needle carries the germs from one drug user to another.

PETS AND PESTS

Throughout history, some terrible diseases have been spread by animals and insects. The bubonic plague and rat fever are carried by fleas that live on rats. Rats also can carry the typhus disease germ. When rats are seen in a community, the health department acts fast to eliminate them before they multiply. People used to get tuberculosis from the milk of cows who had the disease. Now dairy workers and cows are inspected for signs of the disease. Also, milk is pasteurized.

It is heated to a temperature that kills any dangerous bacteria and then rapidly cooled.

A killer disease called rabies is spread when animals who have it bite human beings. This disease is rare nowadays because many dogs and cats get an injection that prevents them from getting rabies. Wild animals such as foxes, skunks, bats, and squirrels may carry rabies, however. For this reason, if you live in a rabies area, don't try to tame a wild animal. If you are bitten, the animal should be tested for rabies. If the animal can't be located for testing, you must undergo a series of painful injections.

Certain species of mosquito are real disease spreaders. In many places, city health departments keep track of the number and kind of mosquitoes and test them for signs of disease. You can help lower the number of mosquitoes by not leaving around puddles or containers of water. Water encourages mosquitoes to multiply.

A small bug known as a tick can carry disease also. It can latch onto you and put a poison in your body if not removed quickly. Ticks cannot be pulled off easily. They fasten their heads into your skin as they feed off your blood. One way to shake them loose is to plug in an electric hair dryer and shoot some hot air on the tick. Sometimes covering the tick with petroleum jelly and then waiting an hour will work. When you go into the woods, cover your hair and wear tight clothes. When you get home, check your body for ticks, especially your hair where they might not be noticed. If your dog was with you, check its coat for ticks too.

CREEPY CRAWLY THINGS

Ticks attach themselves to you outdoors. But there are three other crawly creatures that you can pick up almost any place: **lice, pinworms,** and the **itch mites** that cause **scabies.** All are parasites. That is, they live on, and feed on, other organisms (in this case, you). All three used to be associated with lack of cleanliness. But anyone can get them. Scabies is very contagious. Doctors and nurses get it from patients. Scabies is also the hardest to prevent and the hardest to recognize. Lice and pinworms can usually be avoided if you know how.

Facts About Lice

Lice are tiny crawling insects. They can be seen by the naked eye. Lice can live anywhere on the body, but head lice are the kind most likely to be picked up by boys and girls. You can get lice from the comb of someone who has them. You can also get them by borrowing the cap or sleeping on the pillow of someone with lice. You can even get them from a car seat or a toilet seat. Lice travel fast in a crowded place like a classroom. And each person who gets lice probably will spread them to his or her family.

Female lice lay as many as three hundred eggs during their month-long lifetime. They attach their eggs, called nits, to hairs on a person's head. To eat, lice stab a little hole in their host's scalp, and suck blood. Lice cause intense and painful itching. In fact, a person with lice may scratch his or her head so hard it bleeds.

To get rid of lice, you need a special medicine. Sham-

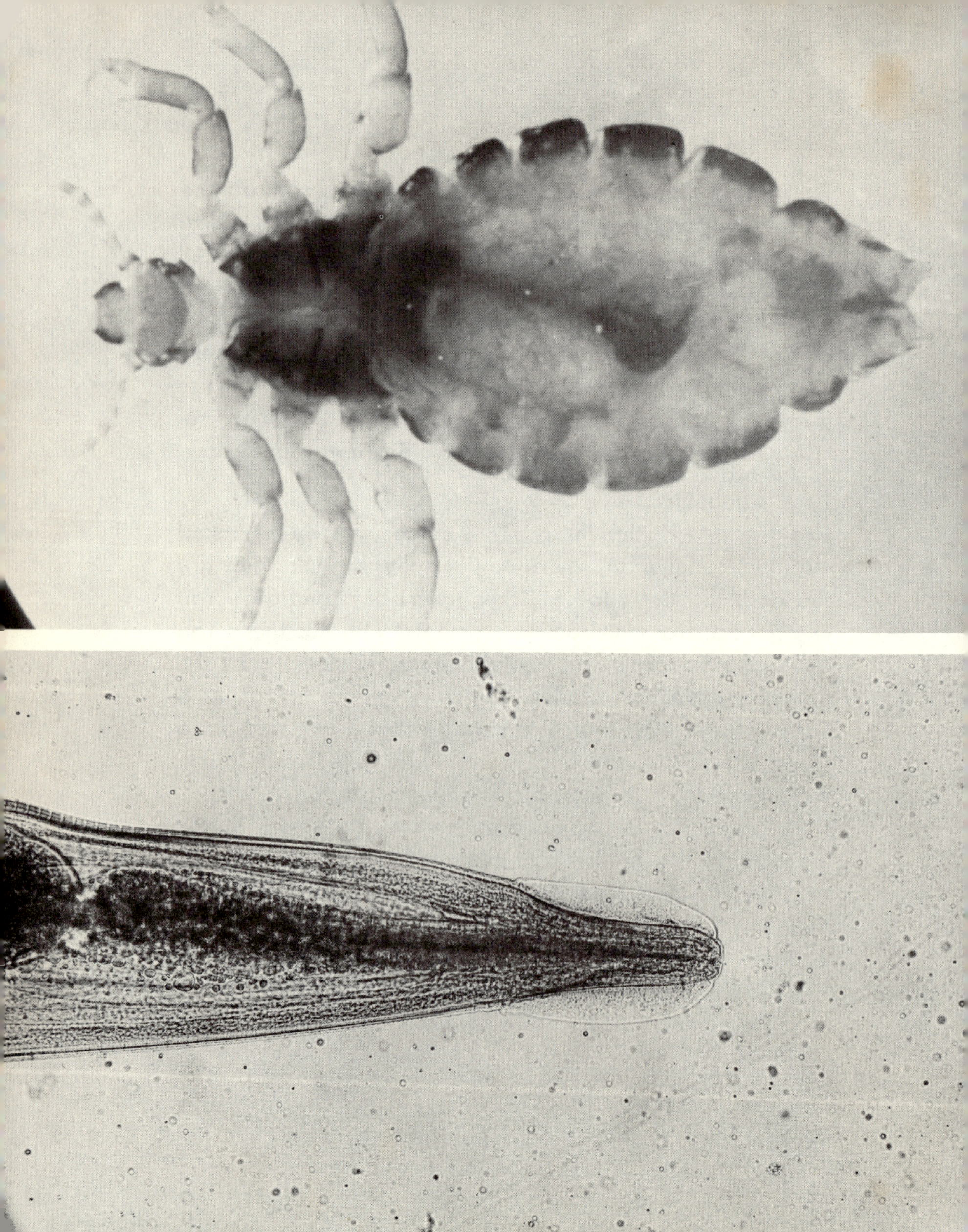

pooing will not kill them. Also, the nits must be removed with a special fine-toothed comb. (That is how the expression "nitpicking" started!) If one person in a family gets lice, special sanitary measures have to be taken in the home. Lice are a terrible nuisance to get rid of. Usually they can be avoided by:

1.   Wearing only your own clothes, hats, and caps;
2.   Not borrowing or lending combs, brushes, pillows, and other personal items.

Preventing Pinworms

Pinworms are about the size of one hair that grows on your arm. They live in the lower intestine of a person infected with them. At night the pregnant female comes out the anus and lays thousands of eggs in the folds of the skin. This causes intense itching. When the person scratches, the eggs stick to the fingertips or get under the fingernails. Then they get back into the body on food the person is eating. If you have pinworms, you must take a doctor-prescribed medicine to kill the worms still inside of you.

Pinworms can be spread easily by very young children who have them. Without knowing it, they can put the pinworm eggs on a piece of bread, for instance, and then offer it to you. Or they can leave a few eggs on a book or pencil

Above: a head louse, greatly enlarged.
Below: head of a pinworm, greatly enlarged.

you will be using. The eggs may stick to your fingers and find their way into your body, especially if you put your fingers in your mouth.

You can see the importance of washing your hands often and of keeping hands, pencils, and other objects out of your mouth. Keeping your fingernails short and scrubbing them with a fingernail brush are two other ways to keep pinworm eggs (and germs) out of your body.

Escaping Scabies

Scabies can be hard to escape. An extremely tiny itch mite burrows just under the skin and produces the rash called scabies. Scabies seems to appear about every fifteen years. In the middle 1970s, many cases of this extremely contagious disease were reported. Scabies looks like a rash of tiny red bumps. In boys and girls, it is found mostly on the skin between the fingers, the inside of the wrist, and under the armpits. It can be found just about anywhere on the body, however.

The rash is extremely itchy, especially at night, when the mite moves around. Personal cleanliness and lots of handwashing do *not* seem to help people avoid scabies if they come into contact with someone who has it. But if you notice an itchy rash, tell your doctor. If it is scabies, you can get medicine for the rash and instructions about washing your

A hand with scabies infection

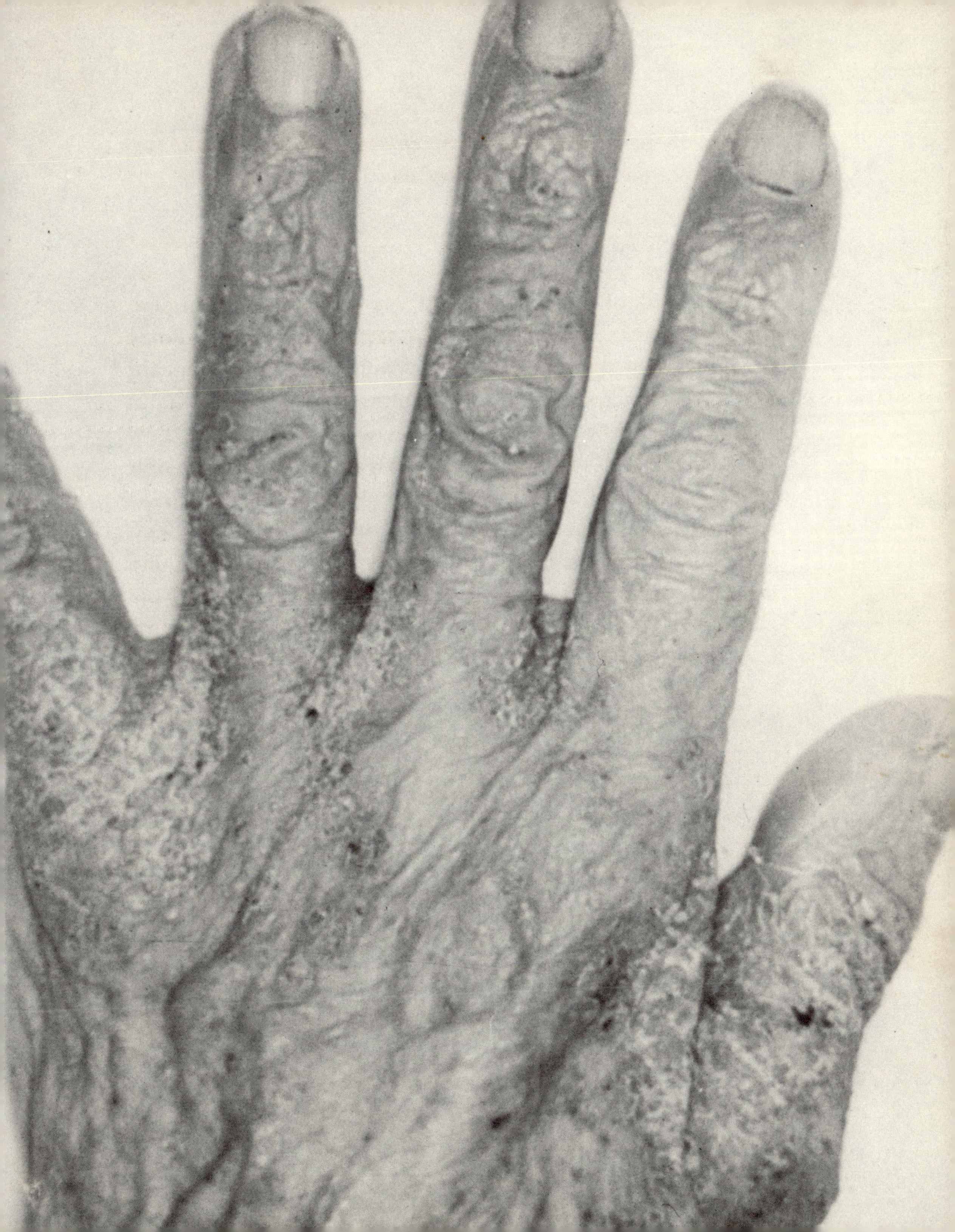

clothes, sheets, and blankets. Since scabies is so contagious, your entire family will probably need treatment.

SHARING YOUR DISEASE

People speak of "catching a cold" as if it were a ball being tossed around. Actually, this is not too farfetched. Some germs *can* travel through the air. When a person with a cold sneezes, millions of tiny disease germs fly out in droplets of moisture. Germs also fly out when you spit, cough, or blow your nose. When you cough or clear your throat, cover your mouth with your hand. Try to have a handkerchief or tissue ready for your sneeze. Used tissues should be stuffed deep in your pocket so they won't fall out. Don't let them lie around the room or drop them outdoors. When you get home, put them in a bag, twist it closed, and put it in the trash can. Colds will be discussed more later.

A sick person should be extra careful not to share food. Always use a separate glass, towel, and pillow. It's a good idea not to ever share these items, even within a family.

CAUTION IN THE KITCHEN

5

One of the most important places to fight disease germs is in the kitchen. You and your family can become sick if someone is careless about the way food is prepared or stored. When you get an upset stomach or diarrhea, you may call it the twenty-four-hour flu (influenza). But sometimes vomiting and diarrhea are not symptoms of the flu but of **food poisoning** or **food infection.**

Food is an excellent environment for germs. Germs need warmth, moisture, and nourishment to grow. A warm kitchen is perfect. The food itself provides moisture and nourishment. In a few hours, an enormous family of germs exist where only a few once lived.

STOP THAT STAPH

Food poisoning can be caused by staph bacteria. This is the same bacteria that may infect a wound. The bacteria can get into chicken salad, for instance, from the fingers of the person who cut up the chicken. Or perhaps the cook sneezes onto the food. Many healthy people have staph bacteria growing in their noses or throats. People with colds have many, many more.

If food with staph bacteria on it stays out of the refrigerator long enough, the bacteria can produce a poison. It is the poison, not the bacteria, that makes you sick. Once the poison is present, cooking the food will not make it safe to eat. Another problem is that staph poison may be present in food that looks, smells, and tastes good.

Before you become alarmed, here is one comforting fact: staph poisoning is easy to prevent. It takes place only when people ignore the basic rules of hygienic food care. One of the most important rules is refrigerating certain foods except when they are being cooked or served.

Staph grows easily in any cooked meat or poultry. Staph also grows quickly in turkey dressing, gravies, in custard-filled cream puffs, and in pies made with milk and eggs. The bacteria are more likely to get into meat or poultry when it is ground, chopped, sliced, or mixed with other ingredients. Some examples are casseroles and chicken or ham salad.

To prevent staph poisoning, remember to:

1.   Refrigerate moist, protein-rich foods, except when they are being served.
2.   Try to keep germs out of food in the first place. Wash your hands before you prepare food. Keep your fingers away from your nose and mouth. If you have a cold or other sickness, don't prepare food.

3.   Handle cooked protein foods as little as possible. Use a big spoon to stir mixtures, not your hands.

4.   Prepare potato salad and main-dish salads (of chicken, ham, tuna, or egg) the day they will be eaten, if possible. Staph poisoning happens more often when such foods are eaten the day after they are made.

5.   Throw out any leftover foods that could have staph poison. Cooking won't make them safe.

6.   Sometimes staph and other bacteria can grow even in food that is in the refrigerator. This can happen when the food is in a large container. To cool a large amount of cooked food, put it into several shallow containers. That way the cold air can reach the food faster.

UNINVITED GUESTS

When you come home from the supermarket with raw turkey, chicken, meat, or eggs, you are probably bringing some **salmonella** bacteria into your kitchen. The bacteria may have been in the intestine of the cow, pig, chicken, or turkey from before it was slaughtered. Salmonella make you sick only when the living bacteria are taken into your body. Salmonella sickness is a food *infection*, not a food *poisoning*.

Adequate cooking kills salmonella. Why then are so many cases of salmonella infection reported each year? People get it when:

1.   They undercook meat and poultry (or eat them raw).
2.   They do not refrigerate cooked food quickly.

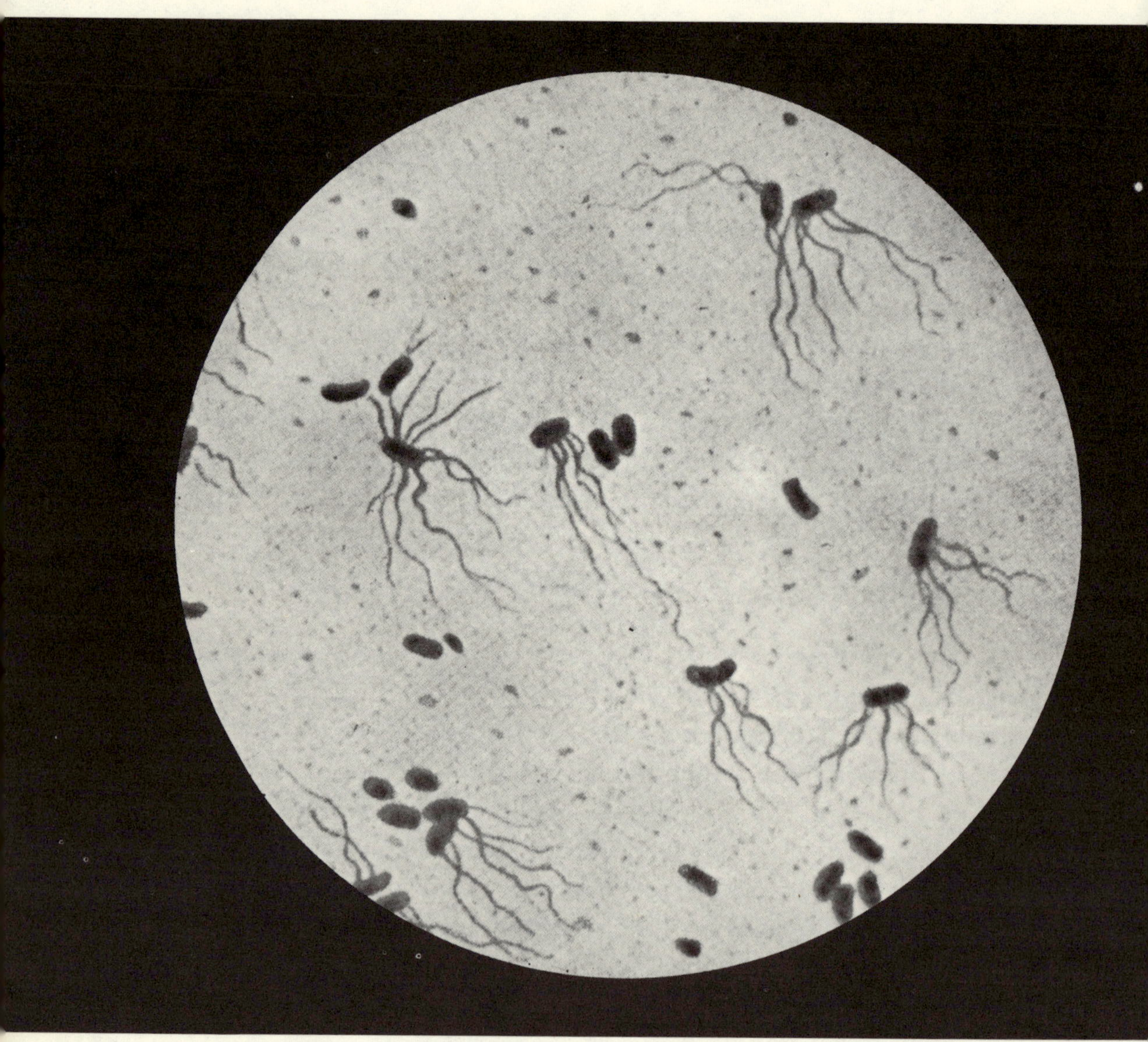

Salmonella bacteria, greatly enlarged

3. They move salmonella from raw meat or poultry to foods that won't be cooked. This is called cross-contamination.

Cross-contamination can take place on a cutting board, a utensil, or a countertop. Any object that touches raw meat or poultry should be washed with soap and water before it touches another food. After making hamburger patties, for instance, wash your hands before handling other food.

Eggshells often carry salmonella. The egg itself seldom does, unless the shell is cracked when you buy it. Some say to throw away cracked eggs. Other experts say they are safe to use in something like a cake, which is well cooked.

Since pet cats and dogs can carry salmonella in their intestines, you should wash your hands very carefully every time you handle your pet or its equipment. Packaged dry dog foods may contain the bacteria. Therefore, wash your hands after you pat your dog or feed it, especially if you are going to eat or prepare food.

MAYONNAISE MYTHS

Mayonnaise is often blamed for food poisoning. The truth is that commercial mayonnaise (made with oil, vinegar, and egg) can slow down the growth of staph and salmonella bacteria. To be effective, plenty of mayonnaise must be used. A little bit does not protect the food. And the food still must be kept cold.

If you take your lunch to school, you can never go

wrong with a peanut butter sandwich. It can sit in a warm room all day and still be safe. But you can also take a safe meat sandwich. A slice of meat slathered with mayonnaise or mustard is safer than a slice of meat alone. But the sandwich must be kept cold. Make it the night before and freeze it until you leave for school. Or make it the night before, refrigerate it, and then put it in a lunch box with something frozen. This could be a can of frozen soda pop or a plastic container of ice cubes.

BEWARE OF BOTULISM

The most serious kind of food poisoning is, fortunately, rare. This is **botulism**, a sometimes fatal disease. It is caused by bacteria that can live and produce poison without air. Most cases of botulism are caused by improper home preserving. Anyone who preserves food should follow exactly a set of recent instructions. These can be obtained from a home economics teacher or from university food specialists.

Commercially canned foods rarely cause botulism. Once in a while, the bacteria do survive the high temperatures of the commercial canning process. A bulgy can means bacteria are alive and producing a gas. If you find a bulgy can, don't open it. Take it to the store manager. Botulism poison can be present without making the can bulge. Never eat or taste canned food (or any food!) that doesn't look and smell as you think it should. Never use food from a leaky can either. When in doubt, throw it out.

SIGNS OF SICKNESS

Symptoms of staph poisoning may appear from two to four hours after eating the food. Nausea and vomiting usually occur, sometimes followed by diarrhea. Salmonella sickness may not show itself until eighteen to thirty-six hours after you eat. Diarrhea and stomach pain are usually the first symptoms. These may be followed by vomiting and fever. With botulism, alarming symptoms such as dizziness, double vision, or paralysis may occur within twelve to thirty-six hours.

A doctor's help may be needed with any suspected food infection or poisoning. Botulism requires immediate action. But other food-caused illnesses can also be serious. Your body, in getting rid of the offending bacteria or poison, can become weak and dehydrated. Dehydration is a serious condition caused by an excessive loss of liquids from the body. To avoid it, you should take it easy, sip liquids, and get medical help if your symptoms continue more than a day.

OTHER HINTS FOR KITCHEN HELPERS

After Shopping

Refrigerate immediately meat, poultry, fish, dairy products, and any delicatessen items, cream puffs, or éclairs. Frozen foods should go in the freezer. Never let groceries just sit in a warm car.

Table Setting

When you set the table, keep germs in mind. Hold utensils by their handles. Don't touch the parts that go into the mouth. Glasses should be held on the outside, plates by the edges.

Dish Washing

If it's your turn to do the dishes, remember to use hot soapy water. Rinse everything carefully. Don't forget the cutting board. Change towels and dishcloths often; they are a perfect breeding ground for bacteria.

Pox on Pests

Wipe all counter surfaces, the table, and the stove, and then sweep the floor. Put the garbage in a can with a tight-fitting lid so animals can't get in. Garbage lying about encourages rats, a serious health problem to you and your community. In the winter, mice are attracted to warm houses with delicious crumbs on the floor. In the summer, uncovered food and dirty counters can attract flies. Their sticky feet and hairy bodies can carry several kinds of germs into your kitchen and onto your food.

HOW YOUR BODY FIGHTS DISEASE--AND HOW YOU CAN HELP

6

YOUR NATURAL DEFENSES

Your body is always on the alert for unfriendly visitors that can cause disease. As mentioned earlier, white blood cells protect the body when germs get inside by way of a cut. But this is only one part of your body's "natural defense system." The hairs inside your nose, for instance, trap many bacteria you breathe in. Your nose and the saliva in your mouth and throat contain a moist substance that kills some bacteria. This same substance is in your tears. When you blink, a thin film of tears moves over the front of your eyes. This washes away dust particles and kills bacteria. Some bacteria on your food are killed by acids in your stomach.

Another natural defense is your body's ability to produce substances known as **antibodies.** Antibodies form when an invading germ enters the body. Each antibody works against one kind of germ. For instance, when you get chicken pox, your body produces chicken pox antibodies. If the same virus enters your body later on, the antibodies will attack

(53)

the virus before it makes you sick. That's why people get chicken pox, and certain other diseases, only once. When your body has antibodies against a disease, you have **immunity** to, or protection from, that particular disease.

THE EASY WAY TO IMMUNITY

You can become immune to some diseases without ever having them. As a baby and young child, you probably received a series of immunizations, or shots, against diphtheria, whooping cough, tetanus, rubella (German measles), rubeola (red, or ten-day, measles), mumps, chicken pox, and polio. You may remember that the injections hurt. Today doctors use very small, very sharp needles that hardly hurt. The **vaccine** the doctor puts into your body, actually containing some of the disease germs, encourages your body to produce antibodies. Thus, the antibodies are already there to protect you *before* you get sick.

Because many babies and children receive immunizations today, some dreaded diseases are not as dangerous as they were. Smallpox, in fact, may soon become the first disease to be wiped out completely because of immunization. But cases of these diseases do still occur, and getting them can be dangerous. If you have not had *all* the immunizations mentioned (plus a simple skin test for tuberculosis), it's not too late. Remember, this is the best way to avoid some serious sicknesses.

Vaccination being given to
prevent smallpox in West Africa

COLD AND FLU GERMS

If you are like most people, at least once a year you are sick with something called the **common cold, influenza** (the "flu"), or a virus. Actually, colds, all types of influenza, and many other diseases are *caused* by extremely tiny organisms called viruses. Viruses are much smaller than bacteria. They are so small they were not seen until a really powerful microscope was invented around 1940.

Some very bad viral diseases such as polio can be prevented by immunization. Immunizations are also available for a few influenza viruses. But it is not possible to prevent most of the types of flu that make so many people miserable every winter. And no one has ever discovered a way to prevent or cure the common cold.

When you have a virus, all you can do is treat the symptoms. Your doctor may suggest medicines to relieve your fever, cough, or stuffy nose. But the medication will not attack the *source* of the infection. Your body has to fight the enemy virus by itself.

Drugs do exist though that help you fight disease. They are known as **antibiotics.** But antibiotics work *only* against diseases caused by bacteria. The medicine kills the dangerous bacteria. When antibiotics were first used in the 1940s, they worked so fast they were called "miracle drugs." Today some bacteria have become resistant to some antibiotics, and the drug won't always work miracles. Nevertheless, they

Influenza virus, greatly enlarged

do prevent complications of a sore throat caused by strep (see later) bacteria. Antibiotics also prevent serious complications that used to follow ear infections.

Sometimes your doctor will say your sickness is caused by a virus but you still get an antibiotic. This is because the doctor thinks that the virus will weaken your body and make it easy for staph or other bacteria to start another sickness. The name for this is secondary infection. An example would be someone who often gets an infection in the ear along with a cold. Antibiotics help prevent secondary infections.

HOW YOU CAN HELP

Whether bacteria or viruses are making you sick, you can help yourself by resting and drinking liquids. When you rest, your body produces more antibodies to fight the disease. Drinking liquids will keep your throat moist, help prevent dehydration, lower your fever if you have any, keep your mucus thin (so your ears and sinuses don't stop up; thin mucus is easier to blow out your nose or cough up and spit into the toilet), and flush germs out of the body. The liquids can be water, juice, soft drinks, jello, or soup. Milk seems to encourage mucus formation, so it is better not to drink it when you have a bad cold.

Blow your nose gently

Don't ever pinch one side of your nose shut when blowing it in order to produce more mucus. Sometimes a vigorous blow will force germ-filled mucus into your middle ear. This can cause an ear infection, or even blow out your eardrum.

Keep your germs to yourself! You know how germs fly out when you sneeze and cough. Cold and flu germs are carried in the mucus you blow from your nose and in the saliva in your mouth. Use your own drinking glass and don't let your used tissue or handkerchief lie around.

When you have a bad cold, don't go to school. You help yourself (and others) by spending a day in bed. Of course, if you are running any kind of fever (when your temperature is more than 98.6° F. or 37° C.), you should not go to school or anywhere else. You also may need to call the doctor.

WHY SOME PEOPLE GET SICK SO OFTEN

Some people get sick much more often than others. In a classroom, a flu germ may be making the rounds, but some boys and girls do not catch it. Why does a disease germ successfully attack one person and not another?

Some people may be resistant to a particular germ because they have already had that sickness. And although there are exceptions, usually a person in top physical condition will have a better chance of fighting off disease germs.

Take the **streptococcus** bacteria. This common trouble-maker causes the familiar strep throat, a disease with possible serious complications. But strep bacteria have been found in the noses and throats of some healthy people. Apparently these people just play host to the bacteria, unless their resistance becomes lowered.

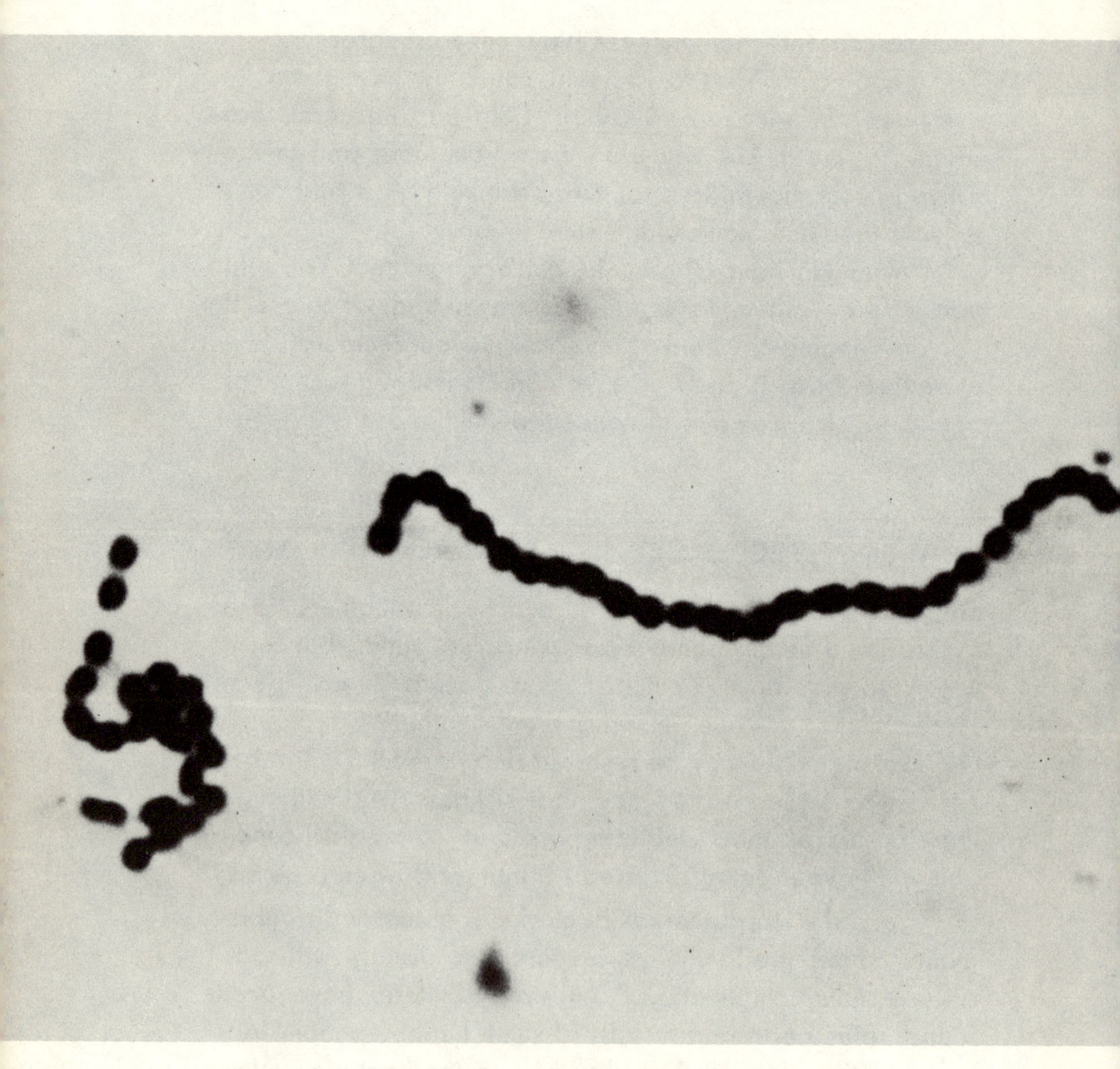

Streptococcus bacteria, greatly enlarged

Medical scientists believe that strep throat and other diseases are more likely to strike people who are overtired, poorly fed, or weakened by another disease.

MAKE YOUR CELLS STRONG

Your body is made up of millions of cells. The cells of your skin, heart, lungs, bones, and all of your other body parts are constantly dying and being replaced by new cells. To grow healthy cells, your body depends on you for nourishment.

Every day you need several foods from each of the following four groups:

1. Milk, butter, margarine, cheese, and ice cream
2. Meat, fish, poultry, eggs, dry beans, and nuts
3. Breads and cereals
4. Vegetables and fruits.

You have heard the expression "junk foods." These foods include soft drinks, potato chips or crisps, and many desserts, especially packaged store-bought snack foods with lots of sugar. Junk foods do these things to you:

1. They give your body little or no building material to produce new cells.
2. They ruin your appetite, so that body-builders such as fruit and salads do not appeal.
3. They encourage tooth decay.

Most of the food you eat should help your body grow.

Healthful food also makes your skin look better and makes your hair and eyes sparkle. And good food gives you energy.

TWO OTHER BODY-BUILDERS

To be strong, bodies need more than good food. They need enough sleep. Because you are growing taller and heavier, your body has to grow more new cells now than it will when you are older. New cells form fastest when you sleep. During that time your body's energy is spent making new cells instead of being used to run, eat, play, and think. When you sleep, your muscles are relaxed and some of your brain activity slows down. The next day, both your muscles and brain are ready to work again.

Regular exercise is as important as sleep. When you exercise, your heart and lungs work harder and grow stronger. To exercise, you don't have to be an athlete. You don't even have to "do" exercises. Walking briskly and running are good ways to strengthen all your muscles, including your heart and lungs. People who exercise discover they have more energy for other activities. When their hearts and lungs are strong and healthy, they don't get tired as fast.

These, then, are the basic rules of good hygiene. You might make a list of those you know you won't remember or don't follow as a habit. Tape your list up—in the bathroom, in your bedroom, even on the refrigerator door in the kitchen. Remember, good hygiene encourages good health, and perhaps even more important, feeling good about yourself.

INDEX